WHAT I GOT FOR A DOLLAR

WHAT I GOT FOR A DOLLAR

*

POEMS BY BERT STERN

Off the Grid Press

Boston, Massachusetts

Off the Grid Press is an imprint of Grid Books.

Grid Books
86 Glendower Road
Boston, MA 02131

www.grid-books.org

ACKNOWLEDGMENTS

Thanks to *Bagel Bards Anthology, Ibbetson Street, Constellations*, and *Salamander* for publishing several of these poems.

A lot of people have encouraged and helped these poems. Thanks to my workshop friends Anna Warrock, Wendy Drexler, Michael Mack, and Rob Arnold. Special thanks to David Ferry and Richard Fein for brotherly generosity. Without my wife, Tamlin Neville, I'd have long since blown away in the wind.

Front cover: "Phasianus," 2010, photograph by Peter Stern.
Printed by Thomson-Shore, Dexter, Michigan. Book design by Michael Alpert.

ISBN: 978-1-946830-01-2

This book is for Ida Jane.

TABLE OF CONTENTS

FOUR

Behind the wind,
something pushing
things around.
Behind the ripples
in water,
behind old age,
torrents of spring
plunge down mountains.

Under my face
I crave another face,
as if behind it all
a God still sleeps,
as if behind the word.

ONE

ON THE AUSABLE

Windy rush of river after rain.
I wobble down the rough path
of the bank, propped by love
and a broken stick, eyes
agog with dappled water.

On the cobbled beach
totter over stones,
breathe beginnings in:
sun, stone, water, rock.

LITTLE PRAYERS

You say wind, rain, sun, moon.
Clouds you say and snow too.
You say bitter cold and delicate
first flowers of apple trees.
You keep saying, child,
beloved, autumn with its
tough promises. You say
currents in the river
you've fished, and earth
laid out like a banquet table
from a mountain top.
What else can you do?
You say breath.
You say death.

MAGPIED MAY

Same old ding-a ling, birds do sing, same old
crocus heads about to resurrect, and daffodil.
Welcome to fresh leaves of Japanese maple,
bronze cavaliers.

Then roll over—goddamn, snowing again
already? Or was it snowing all along? Get up
and back to bed, breakfasting on delicious
dinner, chicken! chicken! chicken!

But the leaves are gone so tell me *ubi sunt?*
So this is old age, like a skunk drunk
on fermented apples. Look out,
here they come again—the leaves.

THERE'S NO OTHER WORLD THAN THIS

Late afternoon in the valley, gangster crows
chase a thrush across the meadow, then, silent,
vanish in woods.

I don't know what goes on back there,
but soon some crows cross back
and crows call back and forth
on both sides of the river.

I'm left with the dark mountains,
still visible through mist, and rain,
as I rock on the porch, pattering
on the roof, then pouring in gushes
to swiftly sodden dirt.

The big pines have been through this ten thousand times.
They take what's given to their neck of the woods,
framing the meadow loosely and carving out
of thickening mist a room that draws me in.

I am so naked I have no skin.

TREES AND I DESCENDING

O dear, it's night, wrapping
its swarthy cloak round
blushing day. *You want it plain?*
day fades to night.

Whatever, something
swallows trees in a slow gulp—
and the trees descend

the path that Orpheus took,
then climbed back up to sorrow
and wild death.

Soon, I'll follow him
halfway. To banish the thought
I shut down my heart and stick
to homeboy sense:

the steady hammering of roofers,
young lovers chatting down the street,
light breeze that ruffles leaves.

Once, before Hitler, we were boys
running like deer in Keds. I long
for the mother who held me close.

Back home, I listen to the branch
tip-tapping on the window pane.

THINGS WHERE THEY SHOULD BE

I'd been sitting by the river all afternoon
and now the sun was going down and Venus
shone on the horizon. I'd been sitting
to watch how the water swirled into braids

and swirled out again. I was watching
a leaf ride the river until, drawn into
sluggish water near the bank, it rested.
Evening fell but the full moon made
          moving water sparkle.

Quite late a trail took me up the long bank
and across a rough meadow home. But before
I climbed the porch steps I stopped and listened
to distant water and a single owl.

Above me Orion was still in place,
so I went in to sleep in a room whose floor
was earth and whose ceiling was moonlight.

All night as I slept, in generous swirls
the river pursued its intricate dance,
as if it were still learning.

VARIATIONS ON SCRITCHING SPARROWS

1

Dim light. New leaves mere silhouettes.
So I'm left with sparrows chirping.
Who knows what they say in their endless
four-beat repetitions? When cars roll by
they're going somewhere. But sparrows
could be rain dripping from eaves,
or something like the sound the sun makes
when it rises, a message not meant for us.

2

Scritching sparrows, or mockingbirds
for all their melodies and car alarms,
have nothing more to say than
un-oiled latches screeching,
Is there a poem like birdsong,
scritch or self-delighting melody
muttered into its own beard,
unable to imagine a listener
as it hums its secret music?

SCANT

Dear dust in which I'll be infinite,
will there be left in you an ort,
a single scant of me, a fingernail
or yellowed tibia to remember
lips that spoke, hand
that holds a pen, path
of puzzlement that brought me
here to address you?
One day, will I fall on my loved one
as rain? At night, standing
on wet grass, will she find me
in the winking light of an orphaned star?

WHAT I GOT FOR A DOLLAR

Something's aching now, as if we're too late.
Skyscrapers are ruins of an ancient city,
we drive on the cracked asphalt of our own dreams.
What rises to the top rises from an underground
we thought was a myth, but now darkness visible
is our president.

Meanwhile, back at the ranch, the man in the Red Sox cap
who loves Jesus (it says on the button pinned to the cap),
offers to help me lug groceries, and though, upstairs,
I give him a dollar
he doesn't do it for that because, when I look for another one,
he waves it off.
"This works," he says, so I know he really loves Jesus.

Contra my argument, love looks out, waiting for us to notice.
It's springtime, and all the swelling renewal is like love.

I try to imagine a time after money, after celebrities
have stopped shouting
and the words a child says as I walk hand in hand with her
sound like salvation: timbre and innocence and openness
to what's to come.

So I know that the world must turn and be worthy of the child—
but so slow, so slow it may not be moving at all.

DAHLIA

Through a bright afternoon
the surf rolled in to sing
the song you first heard
before you had ears, then
it lay white, fizzing, until
the next wave broke.
The children loved
the joke and ran to it,
danced there, pursued it,
and hauled it away
in fragile pails to invisible
holes. All afternoon breeze
held steady as an old friend,
as cool as your poem when it
touched me with its petals.

BLOWN LEAF

The past flies back in out of the blue
with phone calls or a letter from a friend
I thought I'd betrayed who says she loves me.

Droplets of memory like flakes of snow
blow toward me on a wind I can't name,
and then away until it's now again.

Your hand in mine,
we forgot the names of everything
to stare at flaring stars,

and, as in a dizzy change of weather,
we drift with them.

*

One night news of my death
will flutter like a blown leaf,
while outside a cloudy sky
laden with snow
takes on a new intensity,
as if storms were flakes of light.

RE THE WORLD TO COME

Here I am at eighty-five,
but ask me about the world to come,
all I can think is: Now it's 12:28,
will I still be on the clock at 12:29?
For me the world to come's already here.

This brings me to another embarrassment:
I've always been immortal. When I
was only a boy, Blake whispered,
see eternity in a grain of sand—
and I did.

Today a harsher mind reminds me,
"Feel the icy breath—that's death."
I know, I know. Yet here I am,
immortal still, as on the day
when I was born.

Right now, heaven's in the turning leaves
against a lead-blank sky—tomorrow,
sunny. Already I miss weather,
but for now it's given to me like grace.

DOE

No news from the steady strings
of a two-day rain or drip-drops
off the eaves.

No news and scant light,
earth and sky gone vaporous—

also the nervous doe
grazing the north rim
of the parched meadow,
looking up and around
between bites. Then

my chair scrapes
the porch I watch from,
and, white tail flashing,
doe's swallowed by woods.

TWO

KINESIS

There is leaning and lying prone, standing erect, drooping.
There is staying in one place and also running and singing
praise to creation as it thrums with our breathing.
Also, there is lying languorous, for sleep or to take pleasure,
rubbing, kneading, caressing, embracing, letting the palm
glide lightly over skin.
These are acts that express invisible energies.
Wash the body, feed it meat and salt.
Children skip out of lightness and joy.
Listening, tasting, hearing, bringing to mind.
In the midst of turbulent waters we have swimming,
drying, lying on sand under the sun from whence we came.
Standing erect, leaning, falling, rising again and running.
Whistling, humming, singing.

Also there is a list of forms uttered *ab nihil,* then washed
by the waters away. Sky, there is sky and earth,
element of fire that gives light and heat, cooks meat,
inhales forests. Volcanoes speak fire through their cones,
which are mouths to them, and cracks in earth's skin make plates
that grind each against each.
Snow will hide the ground, lay mounds,
and the great floods of spring rivers also declare that creation
rests on the rock of nothing.

Rivers of thaw from rivers of ice.
There are no lean days. In silence we hear the humming unceasing,
that unfolding holds us. We nod sagely, scowl, ponder.
In our smiling we are like the angels. There is belching and farting,
burping. Until the spirit departs, our dear bodies keep pulsing,
whether we are staying or leaving, running or standing still.

THE ORDINARY

I'd like to tell you something new
but it's always the same around here:
me in a chair, eyes fixed on a blank
or busy screen or book or window
that lets in clouds and trees, a neighbor's
house across the street, and, steadily but slow,
seasons, the rise and fall of days, brightness
splashing from the sun, darkness speckled
with stars.

The palette's simple as the scene: skies gray
or blue or dappled, rain, snow or nothing falling,
a tree, one tree I've pruned and love
because it's red and green and Japanese and
longest to hold its leaves.

Up ahead a gale's coming in, but the ordinary prow
keeps its nose to the wind.
Up ahead rumbling thunder, visions of shipwreck,
but something sails on, and I'm haunted by
this ghost, this thin aroma
brilliant and concealed.
As if, behind the same old,
a different face looks out
through glowing-ember eyes.

AUBADE

Why is my heart scared
like a songbird crossing
a meadow
under the hawk's shadow?

Crow says this day's all right,
clouds blowing in from the sea
to bring rain,

but I hump in my room,
wrenched from the bliss about me.
Is it the news that clouds the doors

of my perception, or the secret way
that history's printed in my genes—
my mother's pain that I must carry,

or wanting to write a poem that makes
birds fly, clouds move, sun heighten
for spring, and sings killers asleep,

or a dawn song that shines darkened lovers
into smiling day, where they embrace?
My angel was never closer than now,
breathing on my shoulder.

HOUSE

Because a river borders the west
and a mountain ridge to the east, we say,
"This house rests on deep foundations,"
and bask inside in mock immortality.

But turn the page. Walls turn to snow
powder, that sprinkles the meadows, never
mind what season, and, in our generations,
we join them, though remembering

for as long as we can that the fountain
of youth falls where our eyes alight, even
on gathering snow or pathos of the few
brown leaves that still cling to a branch.

We ask, is spring enfolded in winter?
May we trust bulbs to go on sprouting
out of hard ground into daffodils
and tulips? Keep asking until even
the walls of seasons find their own dust.

Until then, we'll embrace one another through
darkening afternoons, snow-snug under covers,
wind and snow blowing across the living room
a floor below.

IT'S LIKE MEMORY

It's like memory, rocking on the porch
amid cloud-shadowed mountains, an unkindness
of ravens calling across the meadow, and, nearer,

boys in pirate suits wrestling on dew-damp grass,
waging duels with sticks, while, off by the shed, men
like memory split logs, sap wafting, sound of the tear.

From a lightened spot in the sky,
God looks down
from his great distance.

I hear Satan sneer, but I don't care.
Everybody knows that something
looks back at us.

GOAT

She left the barn door open and the goat got out.
The sheep stayed in their stalls, dirty wool braided
with twigs and hay.

She missed the goat, so simply brown and white.
Sitting by the fire at end of day, she dreamt it
with a herd in high meadow grass patchy from grazing.

She dreamt herself there, too, sniffing sweet grass.
When the cold comes, the goats descend, winding
among big rocks to be where the wind softens,

and here and there grasses show through ice and snow
that's nearly buried them.

When she awoke, her room was big as the sky
and her goat, when he returned, called her by name.

SLEEPING WITH THE RIVER

I sat on the river bank all afternoon until
the sun went down and Venus shone low.

I sat and watched the water swirl
into braids and swirl out.

I watched a leaf ride, before it was
tossed into sluggish water near the bank.

Evening fell but full moon made
moving water sparkle.

Still half entranced, I scramble up the bank
and across a rough meadow to home.

Before climbing the stairs to the porch I stopped
to listen to the river and a single owl.

When I was sure that Orion was still in its place,
I went up to my bed to sleep in a room whose floor was earth

and whose ceiling was moonlight.
All night around me in generous swirls

the river pursued its fancy dance as if
it were still learning.

SAMUEL PALMER'S TREES

wear
brutal faces, like clouds
stared at too long.

But the gleaners keep their eyes
on the ground, to pluck what's left
from wheat stubble.

Soon darkness falls over them,
but for now it's hard to name what
lurks in this waning light.

I might say "God," but which?
The one who sees all but feels
nothing?

The people are hungrier than
the cattle, who freely graze
amid the wheat still to be harvested.

God can't remember why
he sent creation forth, and
his creatures never knew.

But Palmer knew exactly
what light falls over us,
and he called it holy.

HEADLINE

I like the weather better than the news.
Rags of a tropical storm just hang around
still spitting gales, driving the trees
half crazy, while a gliding gull
tips feathers this way and that
to keep his airy way above
the stolid faces and spastic trees
of my neighbors' houses.
It's practically a field day, loud band
of sirens wailing down the avenue in hot crescendo.
The news keeps deepening, like mud.

The world has sprung a leak, but the wind
that spills from and drives the clouds, and
the leaden light, they're all right. Empires
come and go, and even worlds. Stars go off
and on and planets start to flicker. Big rain's
begun to torrent down as a gale rises.
The weather changes, but not the news.

MOONGIFT

From the other side of summer a raw wind
blows in and the moon lets dark trees cast
shadows like ashes of their burning. Cold
night in a big house, my head full of pointless
woes, but look! Never a moonscape like this.
Newly landed, I'm an astronaut agog,
watching two white-tailed deer
graze on silvered grass.

Somewhere the sea tears away the shore
and leaves come and go as if
in endless crucifixion/resurrection,
but in this moonlight time's stopped,
except for grazing deer, and, faintly,
the moon's slow trek
across a trillion stars.

SCOUT

I put my poem in a coonskin hat
and send it out to scout:
Read their smoke signals,
live on dry pemmican.

Off it went like honey,
in moccasins and deerskin,
following deer trails,
not breaking a twig.

Find signs, I'd ordered.
Of what? it wondered,
Find signs, I ordered it.

It looked up at a cloudless sky.
Nothing moved
but the slow crowns of trees.

Ahead, the trail, an alley through
primordial trees. My poem
looked down: nothing but
dead leaves and duff.

Bored, my poem hummed
Sweet Betsy from Pike, spat
brown juice down
at low-lying flowers along the trail.

When my poem returned,
bearded and gaunt, it saluted me
Sir, nothing to report. But, pressed,
it fleshed that out, and this was enough.

DOLLY

Darling, the sunny hills are ripe with you.
I smell you in the sweet grass. To the
Dalai Lama you say, "Hello, Dalai," and
he replies, "Hello, Dolly."
Is it because you wear my love that
you are so radiant? No, what do I know
of love except what you taught me.
Now, when I look into the mirror,
are these my eyes or yours?

ELEGY

The going is more like stopping,
the stopping is like dying.
The robin doesn't know this
so he sings anyway. Worm
sighs, *ah well*. Shelterless,
the smitten shiver, staring
at calm sea. The bear doesn't
know this so he stirs.

WEEPING GIRL

Grief rides her, grinds her.
If she would look at the blue veins
in her hand, if she would run
her fingertips over them.
If she would go outside
and start counting leaves
that rock and bounce
breathing in the sun.

Summer will be here soon
and after a while the leaves
will grow old.
Seasons pass.
But the girl still sits
on the edge of her bed.
Empires will rise and fall
but she won't stop crying.

If her mother would come.
If she had a lover.
In time, the sun goes out
but she's still crying.

MORE PUTRID & MORE PURE

Shall I babble brookwise in my late years,
knowing there's an asteroid
locked in on my head?

No, I stand with the encrusted, the lying low,
with root vegetables happy to be left alone
or pulled up in a wink.

Once I heard the thump of my own footsteps.
Joy made a giant of me.
Earth shook in glory.

Now the hushing tide ebbs into
the darkness of a seaside evening.
Here and there

a last spark touches the tip
of a receding wave.
Hear the sand hiss.

So I bring home the bacon of my days.
What's sizzling in the pan?
It's me, older than my zedas,

done almost to a crisp.
Young, I said we were rats in Satan's alley.
Drunk with Baudelaire, I longed to learn

the putrid from the pure.
Now I'm my own remains,
at last pure, and putrid soon enough.

ADIRONDACK EVENING

Watching you from
the second floor of the darkening house
as you cross the meadow and disappear
into the woods at evening,
for a moment I think
I am watching myself vanish into the woods,
but no, I am watching us both
just when our absence from meadow
and woods leaves behind a whisper
like a puff of pollen in the wind
that dissipates on grass and evening peepers
and washes away in rain
and leaves aches in the ether
for the meadow you walked across,
the woods you entered,
my ache for you and yours for me.

THREE

LATE CAPITALISM

I got the last box off the shelf but it was empty.
No mouse holes or telltale top torn open,
just the sealed box, empty when I shook it.

At the meat counter, more of the same:
feathers for chickens, and for swine
the slop that fed them.

I thought *depilatory*, I thought
old men shrinking in their bones.
April past, then the summer gone.

Meteors stop for lunch, the wheel
grinds to a stop. Here and there,
like detritus, a man hammering,

a young girl singing down the street.
Above, storm clouds scudding north,
the bewildered jet stream strayed

from its path, sunshine pale and lethal.
You are watched by seventy-eight eyes
that love you after their nature.

You are a blind and frightened mouth
that believes what it is told and eats
what it is given. Babylon, give us

back our open sky and constellations,
our fiery courses, our bloom in language
that opens and closes like a rose.

DECEMBER POND

It's okay when I'm deep asleep, or when I'm holding you.
But winter-long peaks of snow still sat asquat and grew
in sallow light.

As when we couldn't hug but climbed a rocky trail
to a half-frozen pond, and watched dead reeds
sway like souls tossing in wind?

Back then we couldn't kiss and thought we'd be like this
forever, like winter. But where we sat under winter aspens
that leaned toward the pond, we watched until desolation
wasn't ours anymore but a gift from pale sun and season
that lightened us by freezing us into the scene.

Now, though we're nested warm against the heart of winter,
and, when I touch your hand, young snowdrops with their petals of hope
blast through winter's last dregs.

DUBIOUS DOBBIN, TAIL HEAVY WITH BURRS

Once valiant, mane flying like water
as you ran like rolling wave, trudge for me now
as if for a last time before retiring to clover
fields and feedbags full of oats.

Drag this cart loaded with boards
over frozen, rutted fields and scattered rock,
first to the river where you'll drink from a hole
in the ice, and then to the meadow
at the center of daylight where
I want to build.

You, who were there before
the first rain, and will trudge on after
the last star goes out.

ELEGY FOR TAYLOR STOEHR

Last night as the sun went down I thought of you,
or not so much of you but of how long since we talked
the way we used to, doing each other good.

Ready for bed, I ached for another chance to hear you
and almost dialed, though I knew that the line was dead.
Do what I will, absence is absolute.

Except when I talk to you as now, as if, as if, and hear your voice
the way we hear voices of those who have gone before,
as we follow.

Last time we talked you said you'd come back in
dreams if you could. And tonight, I dreamt you were walking
away down a riverbed, though you heard me when I called.

DEATH MENU

For *hors d'oeuvres* I'll have: waning strength,
shed teeth and hair, fog in the head and body
aches. And for entrees. . .

Of course there's stuff I will not eat:
"Slow and painful, no sides," or
"witless and immobile far too long."

Big *no* to ALS that took dear John away,
and to cancer in its many masks. In the end,
COPD most probable for me, but never mind.

Finally, with a sigh I tell the waitress,
who's dressed in black, "I'll have
'Home in bed, my loved ones
all around me,' please.
And hold the rancor."

STIFF WIND

A wind roars down from the dire northeast
to blow in legumes and leg bones, pickles
and pine trees, the whole nine yards
of frantic birds, along with human
hearts humbled by birds and the sky
above them.

Detritus of grieving mothers
and lost boys feeding on barley
darkens the sun, so too flying barn boards
and the cattle they sheltered.

Mouth agape, I watch weathermen
sucked in with the rest but still
reporting. As I am doing now,
unable to say whether I sit
in my living room or

am wafted outside, pelted
by flying bricks
from somebody's
shithouse.

TURF

Not much of a lawn but he's watering it,
in shorts and a worn blue t-shirt that
barely covers his belly. Poor chap,
poor chap, I'm thinking as I pass.
The grass patch might be all he had
but he was glowering at it.
On his front door, I swear,
three "Keep Out" signs.

CELAN

After typhus took his father and his mother was shot,
he kept walking despite the morbidity of his limbs
until he found shelter in a bramble patch of language
made diaphanous through the veiled darkness of his soul.

Annihilating words, he flowered toward No One,
having lost everything, even the names.

Creaking wheels of carts that carried the dead
like garbage to holes where they lay together
became the figured base of the music he made.
Stars, falling, left black holes in his sky. Earth
blessed him before it left, carrying rumors
of Eden away with it.

So he cut a branch from a burned tree and cut
fine notches no thicker than hairs, and gathered
berries from sterile bushes and dyed putrid
water with them, and on a granite slab shaped
like a coffin he began a conversation with
everything no longer there.

HOW I GOT HERE, NOW THAT YOU ASK

Hot ham with corn cakes all week long,
then the food went silent and my bed
turned to stone. Nobody asked me to
but I jumped off the edge of my earth.

Out there the gatekeeper said no in flames
but I entered. Silence,
then the din of people talking
never to me.

My socks were wet.
I couldn't sleep
on the stones provided.
I forgot my song.

EDGE

Tired of me, Time left me loitering on the edge
of clanging space, watching astral junk, comets,
and, here and there, novas exploding. I mean
really, why not, I an old man beginning to totter,
dear ego dissolving, forgetting what the fuss was about,

what little's left sighing, *phew, particle flew right*
through me, or was that me, particle and passage?
Maybe I'll like it there, though who'll there be
to like and where's there, if not here,
and as to that. . .

ANOTHER OLD MAN AND THE SEA

Out all day on the water
he doesn't think about the big one.
Out all day on the nearly dead Aegean
he only wants one fish with meat
to make his supper.

All day familiar rocking,
squeaking boards of a leaky dory
faded red and blue, all day blue sea
opening to darkness as if sea
were bottomless mind.

But for him, no memory of losses,
no hope for gains. At end of day,
maybe a bony scorpion fish for soup—
first removing poisonous spine.

If the man had a potato. If he had a carrot
or onion. If he had a potato, salt, oil.
Or else, boil just fish in the one pot,
sip soup slowly with no spoon.

Imagine potato, etc. Or simply, slowly
eat bare soup. Tomorrow maybe a ray,
a spiny lobster, even a mullet. Tomorrow
maybe a potato. Now, sip soup slowly,
now sleep.

OH, DU FU, PLANT YOUR GARDEN AGAIN,

the soldiers are gone for the while,
leaving corpses and turds to fertilize the soil.

Maybe this time, you'll bring in a crop
before they return. But they'll be back,
someone's empire never big enough, mothers
weeping in the birthbed over sons
"who will die in foreign weeds."

Listen, my master, speaking
centuries later, I still hear them
screaming almost outside my window,
the human heart still torn, feeding
on itself.

MY ZEDA'S SILENCE

Forty years after he died I started to hear what he wasn't saying.
He wasn't saying because he wasn't saying. By day he'd ride
in his horsecart to sell fruit and vegetables to poor housewives.
"You're asking a dime?" they'd say. "But look, already it's almost
supper time, with beans that are rotten you wanna go home?
I give you a nickel, you'll have one less worry."

With what he did take home, he made pickles, wine, jam.
Sunday afternoons my mother herded us and the whole *mishpuchah*
to visit. We're all in the living room with cousins, eating what Bubby
chopped and kneaded and baked and simmered all morning for us,
but my *zeda* stayed in the kitchen staring into his tea cup.

Alone and silent, schooled by the Cossacks how to dream big,
he struggled to come to America. But his soul was still in the *shtetl*,
where his friends, slashed or gassed or shot, were buried in pits.
That's where he lived, heart and soul. Only the fruits of the earth
could still warm him.

What he wasn't saying doesn't have a language—just the way he sat,
head bowed over his teacup. The way plums boiling in his vat
reminded him of Kishinev, where the hills were once covered
with plum trees. And the *shlivovitz* he made and drank by himself
reminded him also—nothing left to toast to, nothing to bless.

FOR OUR LEONARD, IN MEMORIUM

I give them up, stale dreams of light.
The light is cradled in the night.
Go down, go down, to hunt
the darkness out. In your
shabby shoes stumble over
stone, in your holy clothes
feel ice run through your bones.
You heard an angel lives here.
Something makes the ice shine,
even in the dark. Never mind
your rhymes, it's not
that time. Be stark.
Your tears can't buy
you anything, why
do you sing?

ROT

Stubborn as a wooden barn but going down
board by weathered board.

Roof gone, rain comes in, rot deepens.
Sky clears, sun gets back to shining.

Sun's serene. But barn goes down
like you and me.

Maybe a stray truck stops to see what's up.
Scrawny man with hammer

takes what planks he can,
drives on again.

Cows once penned there,
now they're gone.

Once I leapt from loft
to straw—still do in memory.

stubborn as a rotting barn
but going down.

ON AN IMAGE OF HALVARD JOHNSON

The lamp in the open window breathes friendly fire,
and someone reads in the room it lights, gentle
and auburn warm. But you're out in the dark street.
At a distance, past the edge of town, car beams
climb a country road. Across the street, a white Civic's
parked under a streetlamp, and a web of light-glazed
power lines dangle toward it from the wooden pole
the streetlight's on.

You're afraid to look at the car.
Why is it tinted green, just as the streetlamp is?
Why is this light so different from the window
light, not warmth here but brazen self-sufficiency?
The car knows what it knows and dares you
to touch it. The street's so quiet you can hear
the moon fall on a poppy field blooming
somewhere else, say Persia, where balconies
and towers of minarets are acts of grace.
But right here, this empty light.

ALMOST

like lines by Franz Klein, almost
something you could sit in, but not here
or anywhere you've been. I don't know
why it's so vivid to me, and that's
okay, it pulls me toward it, almost
like the suddenly strange last tincture
of the leaves, like leaves from somewhere
else, an uninhabited planet we've not
seen yet. Something like that. Almost
like winter coming on, and me so old
I've withered like the leaves. Seriously,
look at my skin.

EMBLEM

Don't ask what he's doing here,
half frozen between two cars
in the chilly lot, half up and
half down, clasping a handle
as if to raise himself, God
knows whether before or after
he took the shit half on the ground
and half on him, his pants down
only to his knees. I'm not here
to blame, but shouldn't he be
the flag at half mast flying
on your street corner or mine?

RAG SONG

My grandfather was in the rag business,
his office, the cart behind his horse.
My mother dusted everyday, holding
rags in her hand or at the end of her dust mop.
I wore hand-me-downs that, when I'd done
with them, were rags. Rags are threadbare
cloth, then something tossed down into
the earth when other uses were exhausted.
One day that gull that cuts the sky
will be no better than a rag, a few
dirty feathers pasted to the sand.
Gorgeous bouquets end in the dump.
I'm still singing, beating out dust songs.

MY POEM GOT LOST IN THE WOODS

and trembled when a shadow stirred, it was just a poem,
what chance against the ravening beasts
that live among the trees? But while it could it ate—
a berry, an almost rotten fruit, some gobbet
of flesh a sated beast had left. And it
grew, it brandished a stick, then found fire,
and built, and lorded over.

FADE

Look. Something's left an egg on a stump in the woods.
Of course you can't be sure, but the egg looks fresh
against the rotting pulp.

Pull the camera back. Now the egg's nearly
out of reach, a smudge of blue on what is still
a stump though smaller.

The space that's left luxuriates with weeds and brush.
After you've left the space will stretch, and *you,*
progressively, will be out of reach.

Then, without nostalgia for egg or stump, you'll not
miss anything, not even this now, when life shines through you—
brilliant late November day, red maple's shriveled leaves
still giving light back to light.

TEARS OF THINGS

I can't wait for sorrow.
I chase after it like a Cossack
after a stolen horse. When I meet
my sorrow we embrace,
and when I fall from sorrow's arms
I'm spiritless as a serf. Head hanging,
I wander with a tribe of beaten wives,
soldiers betrayed, those hollow-eyed, bereaved
and hurt, and workers squashed into dirt.
In such company I learn companionship,
drinking their bitter wine.

TRUMP

If you asked me I'd tell you, a poet
lives on a little of this, a little of that.
Not just flowers, either. If he has to
he'll do fine on garbage, on labels
from cans like a billy goat.

He likes it sour or sweet, hot or cold.
Same with seasons: winter's as tasty
as spring to him, dead leaves falling
as good as green ones opening.

Anything, in short, but this, this formless
thing that trumps the leaves and seasons
and the heart's old loyalties, causes the sun
and moon to fold, blows out all the candles.

PLEASE DON'T SEND HELP

It's all around me already.
Dear trees and flowers,
dear sun and moon and sky,
dear friends I can talk with
about whatever I want to.
Son, daughter, oh so dear,
and wife. And, granddaughter
who's just begun to walk.

I owe this poem to a man
named Phil, who, when I asked
him for his version
of the good old days, said,
when I had my wife and knew
what I had. Dear Phil.

SAILING WITH THE MOON

One leg at a time
my pants go on
and I walk downstairs.

Last night the moon
trudged across the sky
erasing stars, one at a time.

CLOSING TIME

Long after my love songs are throttled by phlegm
and the flame in my heart burns down to last embers,
you'll still feel me smiling on you,
long after the sky has packed away its stars and moons
and marched home like a weary soldier.

Our warmth lasts through miasmas
of politicians, glitters brighter than money.

HOLDING YOU

Once I'd ride home in the dark on my Nighthawk
rattling up a gravel road and over a wooden bridge
and be in your arms. On other nights I'd be in a tent
with you while a storm swept over Ocracoke
and tore our windfly off.

Once, thanks to a generous boss, we slept at the Ritz,
breathing in the odors and basking in smiles
that by rights shine only on the rich. And once,
most beleaguered,
in the woodstove warmth of a house filling up with snow.

How is it, then, that we're here now, grown old, muddling
through, remembering? Did we make the trail
that brought us here, turning accidents into luck,
pulling us half-drowned out of disaster by the skin
of our teeth?

Even when my house is a hole
in stony Adirondack dirt I'll hold you, or,
if I can't, waft a molecule of me your way
from time to time like a valentine.

FOUR

I DESCRIBE

because it asks me to.
Snow falls on mountains,
melts and makes rivers
throw down ice and rocks.
Boom! Boom!

Even in the dark
light falls on things,
though color drains.
Until I say
all cats are gray.

Like Kilroy,
leave a record:
remember
the drunk dancing
his empties back to the *tienda*.
in a line of solemn *indios?*

God sent us here
to see and tell because
back home in the *eyn sof,*
He's nothing and nothing's
all he knows.

REASONS FOR NOT WRITING A POEM

Because it can't suck milk from the breast.

Birds will not land on it.

Dirt tears of cold rivers
      break over mud banks.

No sap in the polished wood.

The rage of brothers
      fighting next door
      shakes my bedroom walls.

I hear war's ramcrackacow
      just as well as you do, but
      war and its dead can't read.

The trees' shush silences me.

Melodies a Syrian woman sings
      while the torn soldier curses his wound
      can't stop the bleeding.

The stars burn all night
      and don't say a word.

Don't ask me if I love you.
      Touch my hand.

REVENANT

for Rachel

Today is white. In dim light
your spirit hovers so near
I can hear you,
though not the words.

Can you hear mine, begging
for a gift from time to make
you whole, who were snatched away
almost before we'd found each other.

Though once, when I lay on the floor
and held you up above me, our smiles met,
and all your unspent life shone like a ruby.

GHOST AMONG GHOSTS,

wander your ghostly path,
as if, as if. Only the sparrow
knows what's what
through ages of saying nothing.

Mountains that stare back at you
stay hidden,
though you try to hint
with a gesture, an expression,
that you're in on the joke
because you know that
green mountains will be gilt
elephants again, and you
in the howda.

RECUERDOS

for Lysander Kemp

Afternoons, on the shores of Lake Chapala,
we watched the rains come in, then sprinted
back to La Quinta for beer at Lloyd's honor-bar
to celebrate our timing. Early evenings, we'd eat
blind whitefish, then, on the patio, breathe in for hours
gigantic flowers, and, rapt with gigantic stars,
sip Campari sodas.

You'd remember the horse I rented that kept trotting
back to the whorehouse, and how the girls in front laughed.
And the village cop, strutting in his Sam Browne belt
who hassled me for papers on the square until Esperanza
drove him off with her sharp tongue. *Sopas* in Tlaquepaque,
long bus rides to Guadalajara. Everywhere,
music and flowers.

But who's to remember with me now that you're on the other side,
first of my friends to die—you, who, before I knew, said I was a poet.

PIG WATER

By starlight the women come down to draw water,
but first they placate their pond, their "Pig Water,"
haunted by demons that pull unwary ones
down by the legs. The women filling their buckets fear
demons but have no other water. One night, while
I slept beside this pond, I dreamt I was one of them,
my *huipile* smelling of me and smoke.

Once I could be anything. I went on and off
with the stars. I dove straight out of the sky
to skewer a pigeon on a chain-link fence.
The world doesn't end at the tip of your nose.
I felt the wind whisper messages at Delphi.
I understood what the cornfields were sighing.

Keep your end up. Comport yourself with dignity,
as the trees do now, in late October, though hardly able
to cling to their leaves under the pounding rain
that cars splash through like children.

STALKING

Hunters don't move in a straight line.
Neither does prey. A turkey hunter
will crawl in the duff all day
for a chance to pop one—and
how that bird rambles.

It's like that for me with this task
I bring only my empty mind.
Crisscross, the turkey goes,
in long curves, low under the brush
where no paths are.

ELEGY FOR HENRY BRAUN

Any man could imagine this:
three friends and you around
a fire, reminiscing, telling
back-then stories and now
ones too. Y'all know one
another deep as the bones,
your shadows playing
on the trunks of old oaks.

Then the silent marauder's
there and you are three,
and now the woods move
in as if—though not yet
doing it—to engulf the fire.
Still, the stories are strong
as oaken roots.

And then you are two.
The woods are darkening
deeper. Love hasn't vanished
but it's grown more ghostly.
On some plane it's true
that you're still five, though
the wind's whistling through
your bones.

Somewhere bereft, children
weep in the night, and wives
toss in beds abruptly unfamiliar.
You two, though more fragile,
feed the fire, until you are one.
This you is you, or—say it—
I, somehow reading silent stories,
as if dead friends were candlelight.

WAITER, THERE'S AN ELEPHANT IN MY SOUP

You call the waiter, who examines, then shakes his head:
"No, no, that's just a tiny tinted tortellini and it belongs there."
But you're not convinced. You pick it up in your soup spoon,
where it taps its right front foot as if testing the water. "Yes,
yes," the waiter says. "Let me get you a fresh bowl." "Look,"
you direct the waiter. "Real tusks." "Yes, yes," he says.

You can't let it go. A living creature flushed down the drain?
Take it home and keep it in a cage? Make a shtick of it:
Sell tickets to the neighbors, go on TV? Become maybe
a celebrity, fielding questions to which you have no answers?
The waiter can't help you, and when he takes away the bowl,
you keep the elephant on your spoon. When your entrée
comes you carefully put the elephant in the salad,
where he grazes placidly.

You pay your check and wrap the creature carefully in a napkin,
and a little salad with him. Your lunch break's over now,
but you call the boss: you're sick and can't get back to work today.
At home, your wife's on the phone and the children (Dr. King Day,
no school) are engrossed in savage interactive video games.
Nobody looks up, even when you show them the unwrapped
elephant on the spoon.

You think the elephant loves you. You read it in those big, deep eyes.
So, all celebrity dreams, or even amusing the family, are out the window.
You build a little cage that also fits the pocket. Sometimes you dream
that if the elephant should die you'd take up scrimshaw. But mostly
you have no secondary schemes. It's all about the elephant
and the infinite peace it gives you.

COMMON IDIOM

She knew and she believed
that a bird in the hand
was worth two in the bush,
and welcomed him as a blessing
in the disguise of being a dime
a dozen and having a chip
on his skinny shoulder.
But, what the hell, she thought,
a leopard can change his spots,
and he might become the apple
of my eye. Isn't he all bark
and no bite? Aren't I working
against the clock? True, his touch
may add no fuel to the fire, but
if not him I'm back to square one.
The choice was dire. Had she
bitten off more than she could chew?
She bit her tongue. Who knows?
He might just cut the mustard.

She crossed her fingers, Onward!
come hell or high water. So she
allowed his arm to slip down, cut
to the chase. Drastic times call for
drastic measures. Before they'd done
it was a flea market: everything
but the kitchen sink. They went
for broke. They went the extra
mile, kept at it all through
the graveyard shift. Idle hands,
now she could reflect, are
the devil's tools. Bravo to that.
As for him, he'd got in like Flynn.

He'd had her in the buff and
she was in the bag. Where this
might go was anyone's call,
but they knocked on wood,
kept their fingers crossed.
Made no bones about it.
Each knew the ropes.

Ah, but love is a New York minute.
No dice in the end. She was barely
keeping her head above water.
In just two weeks she had no room
to swing a cat, and that was that.
She'd been out on a limb, but now
she was off the hook. They pulled
the plug. He never knew what
had queered his pitch. But Rome
wasn't built in a day. For both,
time to start from scratch. To make
a long story short, it was water
under the bridge. And anyway,
variety is the spice of life.

DEGAS' NUDES

I will never be languorous, like poured honey,
and I can't stretch my arms above me to assert
proud flesh. So I hover close to the threshold,
sniffing for an aperitif, a *soupçon.* And then,
voilá, this is me, Venus on the halfshell—
eternal Virgin newly hatched, delighting
nymphs and zephyrs.

Or take one of Degas' nudes, descending to
or ascending from the bath. Sure, for D and me
it's Peeping Tommery, but more: we're being
what we peep at: entering the Other's sexual realm
as eternal solitary, plain flesh luxuriating at ease
in its own languor.

Granted, a woman stepping into the tub
is a woman dissolving in her own heat.
How little she needs me, wrapped in
the water of her pleasure.

Still we crave, Degas and me, to be with her,
to *be* her, to see her having stepped—ah—out
and drying the space between pinky and fourth toe,
with perfect focus that invites me to be the towel
and to be her bending.

A POET DOESN'T CARE

whether he counts sparrows or raptors,
seagulls or songbirds. Like a child
counting baubles he cries, *Ah.*
He cries, *The glittering of the leaves,*
the scurrying of field mice among the sheaves.

And so he goes on, minding his business
like the chickadees do, just feeding,
staying alive,
with luck even through winter.

RIDING BAREBACK IN THE TROPICS

I ate sour oranges and sweet lemons because
this was the tropics. Watch out for coral snakes,
my weak heart told me, and gather psilocybes
for the trek you'll take later, dreaming
of Central Park where the inline dancers mate
like birds in air, then glide off in different directions.

What's not like this? Fluid meetings, wrenching
partings, standing on the bottom step of the
front porch in tears, half pleading, but no,
she lets me go weeping down the street through
dirty blocks to the bus station, and a ticket
to as far south as I can go.

So it came about, all old ties broken,
high in the canopies, spider monkeys noisier
than neighbors, air orchids the horses loved
to eat. One night, drunk, I galloped bareback
round the rim of a great, natural bowl, with only
my thighs to gird me against the unnamed hurt
I somehow managed to keep dodging,
even among coral snakes

This story has no moral, except, the ordinary's
more fragile than you think, and when it tears,
look: clamorous worlds you'd hardly dreamt
stare you in the face.

ABOUT IT

The boy can't look at himself in the barber's
mirror, but there he is, and his face says
he's all wrong. Oh for someone to say
otherwise, but the barber won't and not
his father. Mother loves him but what
those two have together doesn't carry
into the open air. The haircut's all right
but it can't change anything. Even
the barber's all right but his own kids
are more than he can handle.

The boy grows through lots of haircuts.
Just when it feels okay to look at himself
he sees that it's all a con, his face is his face
and so what? But a lingering smudge
in his soul says, not quite, try harder.
The boy thinks, Oh for the hero's life,
slashing my way to glory—or
the devout's, on his knees, appealing
to the heart's desire that waits in heaven.

The heart's desire. Lovers know it
for a moment, the princess and the prince,
while they're fitting slippers.
The birds don't have it but they don't care,
and the trees the same, who sigh their way
through springtime and summer, then shed
what they must—no regrets.

Later, the boy loved a girl and they got married.
After a while, scratched by the usual thorns,
they forgot what love is, but late, though
the fire was banked, they remembered

in one another's arms that love
is what we have. In the eyes' mirror
they gave each other back, bedizened.

FOREVER

Blithely, hands clasped behind us,
we walked a razor's-edge ridge
exactly two miles high. You asked,
"Are we in heaven?" and I said,
"No, not yet." Below us eagles
cruised the valley, below them,
though we couldn't see, we knew
brown bears went grubbing.

You said, "I like it here, even if it isn't."
So much to like: clouds floating
through us, sun so close we could
touch it, and us so free it didn't burn.
You sang a song about how our lights shone.

There must have been a trail down
but we weren't looking. The ridge
stayed sharp as far as we could see.
Somewhere it must dissolve into a slope,
but did we care?

Soaring birds told us everything
they knew about flight, then sang,
"Follow us." We were tempted
but held to our ground. After all,
here my lust and anger dissolved.
What could we need beyond the sound
of boots on granite?

We'd forgotten what forever was,
though it seemed we might be there.

WHEN I HAD LEGS

Running on soft mornings that went on forever,
across the meadow, down the gravel road, along
the river where once a blue heron and I startled
each other, then past the house where beagles
charged me so I carried stones, and down
to the street past the hardware store and up
the steep path to the rich Smith's camp
and along the trail through their fragrant
piney woods to the locked gate you can
walk around, and down the John's Brook
Road with its residual roar that gets louder
as I move toward the falls itself and
stop there, from one side of the bridge
watching the water bounce off boulders
in crescendo, and then to the other,
where it tumbles down over boulders
and is already almost quiet when it
vanishes around the bend.

IDA JANE

My granddaughter's name is Ida Jane
and she makes me fall in love again.
May she say my name forever,
or reach toward me. May she feed
me a cloth sandwich. Let me
live by the light of her smile
for as long as I can.

Co-founder of Off the Grid Press, Bert Stern is the author of two previous poetry collections, *Silk/The Ragpicker's Grandson* and *Steerage*, as well as the critical book *Wallace Stevens: Art of Uncertainty*, and *Winter in China*, a monograph on American expatriate Robert Winter. He is Milligan Professor of English Emeritus at Wabash College, and has also taught at the University of Thessaloniki as Fulbright Professor of English and at Peking University. Stern served as chief editor for Hilton Publishing, and for fifteen years taught for Changing Lives through Literature, a program designed for men and women on probation. He lives in Somerville, Massachusetts.